Illustrator's Note

Ancient Korean culture is the inspiration
for this coloring book. You will be able to
color lively images which depict traditional
Korean clothing, paintings, cuisine, plant
life, landscapes, animals, embroidery,
music, and much more. Exploring this rich
culture and illustrating it along with
imaginative twists has been a very
rewarding experience for me, and I hope
that you will also find the same enjoyment.
Feel free to interpret my lines any way you
wish, and add the colors accordingly.

Coloring Suggestions

❖ There are many ways to color this book, but I would recommend colored pencils, fine tipped markers, and non-alcohol based pens.

❖ If you are using markers or pens that may bleed through, place a scrap piece of paper beneath the coloring sheet to prevent staining onto other pages.

❖ There are no correct or incorrect colors. Blend, stripe, dot, shade and smear anything you want. Go outside the lines. Create surreal images. My lines are not the art. They are the frames.

❖ Feel free to practice here

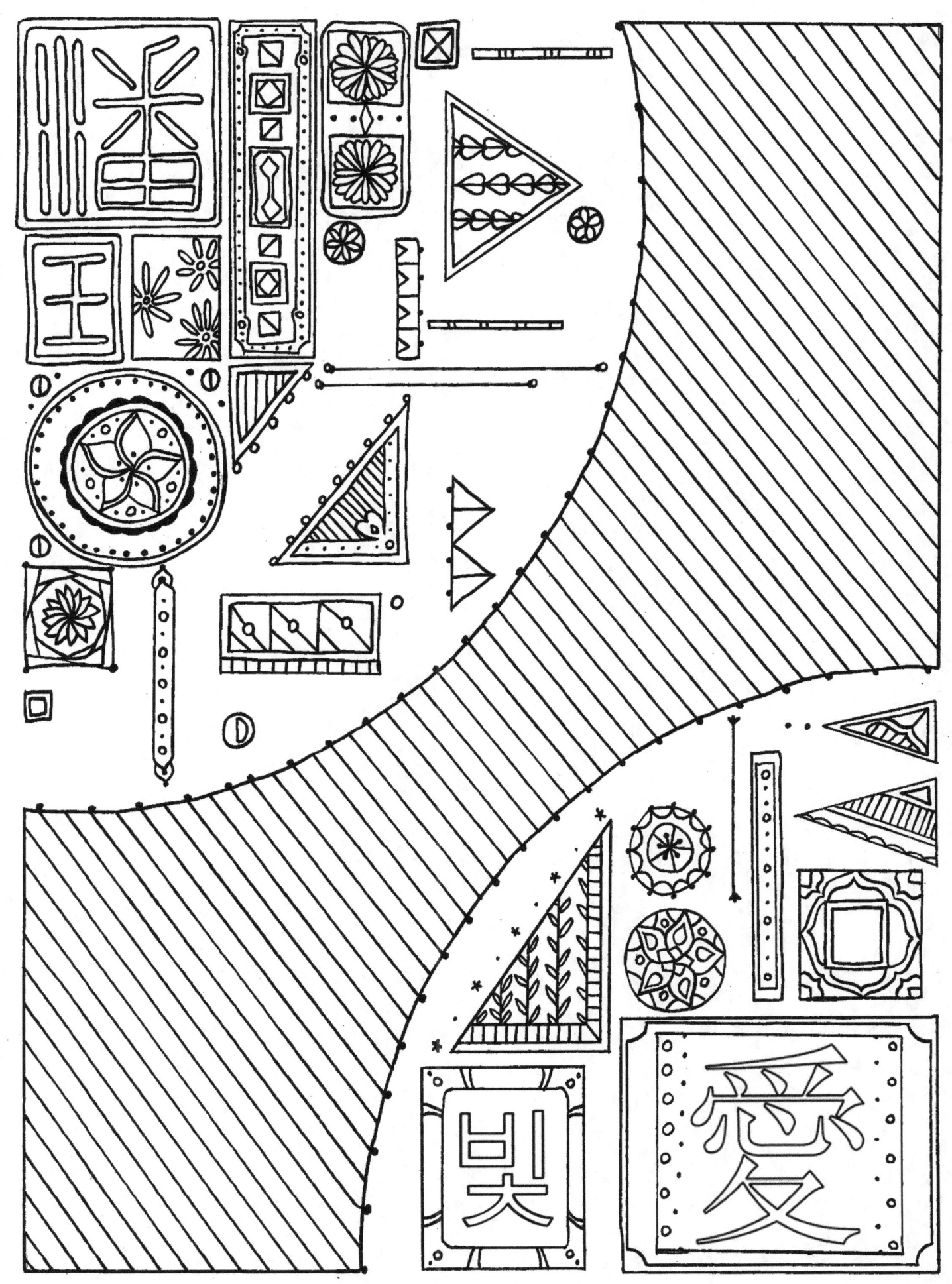

Thank You!

Thank you for purchasing and supporting my work. I hope you have enjoyed coloring my illustrations.

Special thanks to those who have encouraged me on my first published work with their support and motivation.

Also, a huge thanks to my mom and dad, who have supported me all the way through and provided the resources I needed to create this book. Thanks, Mom and Dad.

About the Illustrator

Sheri Guo is an aspiring artist who is currently in her sophomore year at Thomas Sprigg Wootton High School. Being genealogically half Korean and half Chinese, she grew up submerged in the beauty of both cultures, hence inspired to appreciate traditional Korean culture through illustration. Although this is only her first published work, she hopes to create more in the future, in the mission of making people happy.

Contact

sk8fs3@gmail.com